HOLISTIC HEALING

HOLISTIC HEALING

A Comprehensive Guide to Alternative Therapies

B. VINCENT

QuantumQuill Press

CONTENTS

CHAPTER 1

Introduction

The holistic concept in medical practice, which is distinct from the concept in alternative medicine, upholds that all aspects of people's needs - psychological, physical, and social - should be taken into account and seen as a whole. A holistic approach means to support and help the person to be healthy and to reach the best of their abilities. It is therefore necessary to have active participation from the receiver as a whole person in order to achieve the highest levels of health.

Holistic healing is characterized by considering a person's "whole being" - their mind, body, spirit, and emotions - in the quest for optimal health and wellness. It is underpinned by the understanding that every individual is unique with his/her individual requirements to achieve a sense of balance and well-being. It is the viewpoint of the journey that is significant and not the destination. It does not only aim at the non-existence of symptoms or illness but aims to bring a sense of balance and well-being, provided that a feeling of being totally alive and enthusiastic about life.

CHAPTER 2

Understanding Holistic Healing

One model of holistic treatment that is used to diagnose illnesses can be the aetiological model of traditional Chinese medicine. This model attributes every symptom to a root cause, and the symptoms and their causes are interrelated. The chief symptom is not necessarily the main problem; an example here is one person may have chronic hiccups, but it is due to a sickness in the kidney. Each symptom can be linked to a particular cause and a particular organ. This model is used to diagnose the interrelated symptoms and problems and their causes, and provide a complete picture of the person's illness. This Chinese model has a great deal of similarity to the biopsychosocial model wherein it is also believed that an illness or a disorder is caused by a specific event which has led to emotional problems, affecting how a person functions in society with their particular disorder; so on a wider scale.

Holistic healing is actually a way larger subject than what most people might think. When you first hear the word 'holistic', your immediate thought may be 'natural medicine'. To sum it up simply, holistic healing is treating the problem as a whole. Let's put this into perspective: physical ailments are often accompanied by emotional and mental problems. For example, consider a woman who has a heart condition. This woman may also have complex emotions involving her family. She may also have psychological problems associated with physical pain. Although she is receiving medical assistance, her mental and emotional issues are not being addressed along with her heart condition. Holistic healing would seek to treat the heart condition, along with the emotional and mental problems. (definition from a holistic healer)

CHAPTER 3

Benefits of Alternative Therapies

Alternative therapies are often able to give a sense of longer-lasting change to health and increased vitality. This is because they are aiming to influence the underlying causes of the illness with an approach that is more empathetic and uses more extended consultations. Energy-based therapies can be quite effective for improving the overall "flow" of vitality and the function of the immune system, and are often perceived as quite relaxing, even if the relaxation response has been an acute crisis of panic or anxiety. In a randomized controlled trial of Reiki in psychological and depression reported illness, it was shown that the treatment was more effective than placebo in the promotion of health and the reduction of mood-related symptoms. This same sense of relaxation and improved vitality can often be experienced from many of the massage and bodywork techniques, particularly those that are more deeply nurturing and the application of aromatic oils with some form of psychological support.

Probably the most common use of alternative therapies is to seek effective relief from chronic pain or the debilitating effects of long-term health problems. People with arthritis, for example, will often do almost anything to relieve the pain and stiffness in their joints. In this case, acupuncture is certainly worth a try, as the evidence from recent controlled trials suggests that it is an effective treatment when compared with "sham" acupuncture or certain pain-relieving drugs. The main advantage of acupuncture and moxibustion is that they are relatively safe in the treatment of chronic and subacute conditions, as compared to drugs, which often have a range of side effects.

There are many benefits that someone can gain from alternative therapies, and this is what often attracts people to them. However, because these benefits are often quite different from what might be experienced from orthodox medical treatment, it can be difficult to assess their relative value. What tends to matter most for people seeking therapeutic change are the immediate gains to their symptoms or the restoration of health.

CHAPTER 4

Exploring Different Types of Alternative Therapies

Holistic health takes into consideration the whole person - body, mind, and spirit, and integrates a wide range of therapies. The use of alternative therapies is interwoven with this holistic view. The following is a detailed look at several of these therapies and how they fit into the model of holistic health. Note that the description of these therapies is brief and some aspects are simplified for the sake of brevity. A more detailed understanding of each therapy would require further study and/ or experience with the particular therapy.

The last few decades have seen a significant rise in the use of complementary and alternative therapies that fall outside the conventional medical model. Whether this rise is due to an increase in the public's dissatisfaction with conventional medicine, or because patients are taking an active role in their healthcare by seeking alternative care, the willingness of clients to explore alternative therapies presents the opportunity for a more holistic approach to health and wellness.

4.1. Acupuncture

There have been many studies on the effectiveness of acupuncture, particularly for the management of pain. The World Health Organization (WHO) has determined that acupuncture is a suitable treatment for a wide range of illnesses, and it is a good adjunct in treatment to aid in the side effects of diseases to the treatment of those diseases.

The duration and frequency of acupuncture treatments can vary. A simple acute case may only require a single treatment, whereas a complex or long-standing chronic ailment may need treatments over a course of weeks, months, or years. This does not mean that you will need to undergo acupuncture for the rest of your life. It simply means that your ailment may require more treatments to resolve it than someone else's.

Acupuncture is a method of encouraging the body to promote natural healing and improve functioning. This is done by inserting needles and applying heat or electrical stimulation at very precise acupuncture points. Acupuncture points are seen as places where nerves, muscles, and connective tissue can be stimulated. The stimulation increases blood flow while triggering the activity of the body's natural painkillers.

4.2. Aromatherapy

The scent causes mood changes by affecting the limbic system, the part of the brain which controls emotions. This is why aromatherapy is believed to work, because numerous fundamental principles of aromatherapy do seem highly plausible to a Western scientific view. Aromatherapy is presented as a holistic therapy, drawing together psychological and physiological healing. Researchers have shown that odors have an 87% effect on our mood and a 48% effect on our body anxiety. Stress-related problems are a key element in many disorders, and it has been calculated that 75-80% of visits to GPs are stress-related. This is an area where aromatherapy can be especially useful. Studies have provided evidence for the effect of essential oils on stress hormones and the anxiety response in animal studies, as well as a positive effect on mood in a trial involving patients with dementia. Aromatherapy has vast potential to help a variety of psychological problems through the use of scents to change mood and behavior. Aromatherapy has been proven to be a valuable psychotherapeutic tool, as well as being particularly cost-effective due to the high dilution of our oils and, of course, with few, if any, side effects.

4.3. Chiropractic Care

Manipulation of the spine and peripheral joints to improve joint function - that is the definition of chiropractic care. It's quite difficult to understand at first, but basically it's all about joint positions and their movement. Joints are like the ceilings in your house; they have certain positions and ways to function properly. Chiropractic care is like fixing your roof if it leaks or your ceilings if they rust. Chiropractic care has been practiced in many countries. In a survey conducted in 1997 by the National Center for Health Statistics, 29% of respondents had seen a chiropractor. In Canada, 700,000 people had seen a chiropractor, and in New Zealand, the figures were 50% of the population seeing a chiropractor within the last 5 years. From this, we can see that chiropractic care is well known to many people.

4.4. Herbal Medicine

Coherent, referencing connecting directly with the information that precedes and follows it. This section looks at how herbal medicine has been viewed both from within and outside the herbal community and how the changing patterns of diseases and expectations from patients have caused herbal medicine to evolve from the days when the village herbalist was a central figure in any rural community.

Herbal medicine examples are well-documented within all the world's cultures and are seen as involving a spiritual link with the "prana" - the universal life force. Within the philosophy of herbal medicine, both the herbal practitioner's own vital force and the herb's vital force must be in harmony for healing to occur. Herbal medicines are said to act on the body as gently as possible. The medicine aims to aid the body to a state of health in the most natural and least invasive way. This philosophy is a reflection of the doctrine of the mean, as the properties of the herbs are used to counter the ailments in the body in a balanced way and will result in healing by restoring the balance of the patient's humors. The vitalistic philosophy includes the uniqueness of each individual and the concept of constitution. For the above reasons, herbs are used with the intention of treating the person as a whole and are selected on the basis of an individual's pattern of disharmony rather than a specific disease. This idea of matching the "similimum" is in accordance with the concepts described in the Essay on Homeopathy, and its comparison is an in-depth overview showing the similarities of Western herbal medicine and homeopathy. Although herbal medicines are used worldwide, the concept of herbal medicine is changing in current paradigms in different countries. This is discussed in a review of herbal medicine and implicates a need for further studies that determine the efficacy and safety of herbal therapy, with the use of the best research in the design of herbal treatment. This can be further compared in depth with Ayurvedic medicine and its current place in the modern world.

4.5. Homeopathy

Although some remedies can produce noticeable effects within a short period, it is more common to take remedies over a longer period of time for deep-seated chronic conditions. Healing progresses through a series of homeopathic treatment episodes, each bringing further improvement to the patient's condition. This is the concept of improving one's health over progressive levels of healing episodes until a return to balanced health is achieved. Next, the author explains the reasons behind the safety and efficacy of homeopathy, which he talks about before. This begins with an explanation of how the remedies are prepared, which is important to know for this alternative type of healing.

Homeopathic remedies stimulate the body's vital force and are individualized for each person. It is known to enhance the body's own healing process. Each homeopathic treatment takes into account the person's physical, mental, and emotional symptoms before prescribing the correct remedy and helping the patient return to a state of balanced health.

The author starts by saying, "Homeopathy is a natural therapeutic system which has been in use for over 200 years. It is a safe and effective system of healing which assists the body's natural tendency to heal itself. This is a holistic form of treatment which is based on the concept of stimulating the body and mind to work together more effectively." He starts by explaining that homeopathy is a therapeutic system of healing which is effective in treating a wide range of acute and chronic sickness. It is also safe for all ages and is known to help benefit those with weakened immune systems, including the elderly and children. In class, we learned that homeopathy is a safe, effective, and alternative science system of healing the body. Homeopathy is used to treat a wide range of health conditions and is a specific method of treating that looks at the body, mind, and spirit as a single entity.

CHAPTER 5

The Mind-Body Connection

Einstein and Buddha both philosophize that everything is relative, and that includes the mind and the body. This section will offer a comprehensive overview of the various forms of mind-body therapies and how they interface with the disease process. The mind-body connection is a core component of the holistic model of health because how the mind and body interact has profound effects on health and healing. In the Western view, the mind and body were long viewed as distinct entities. This duality is a reflection of Cartesian philosophy, which has had an immense influence on the development of the modern world, but is a disservice to our understanding of the way the world really works. It is this dichotomist view that has led to an alienation of mind from body and, in doing so, resulted in a loss of touch with the many ways in which the mental processes affect the functioning of the organism. In this case, it has been the individual's alienation from his own self with detrimental effects. When the Cartesian philosophy is extrapolated to the extreme, the mind is viewed as a general running in the brain, completely independent of the body, with which it has no essential connection. This simply is not the case and in recent years it has become less and less tenable in light of the evidence from various scientific disciplines. Although a detailed account of the many ways in which the mental processes affect the functioning of the organism is beyond the scope of this essay, a general understanding of the interaction between the mind and the body is important in the context of mind-body medicine. There are a vast many pathways, but we can group them into two general types: the effects of the mental on the physical and the effects of the mind on behavior, which has direct consequences on health.

5.1. Meditation and Mindfulness

Heart-centered meditation is used to help cultivate feelings of love and kindness for oneself and towards others. This is often practiced by taking a comfortable position, closing the eyes, and bringing to mind and repeating certain mantras or affirmations.

Mindfulness meditation allows the meditator to observe the thoughts as they change and become aware of the various patterns and habits of the mind. In mindfulness meditation, the meditator's awareness is open to the experiences of the present moment and is able to detect when the mind becomes drawn into the past or the future.

Concentration meditation involves focusing all of one's attention, energy, and effort onto a single object. In this form of meditation, it is said that the mind is able to transcend the usual stresses of discursive thought and change.

With its roots in ancient contemplative practices, meditation has long been held as a means to spiritual growth and enlightenment. For the most part, the traditions and techniques of meditation are derived from spiritual or religious practices. These techniques have been systematized and are now being utilized for reducing stress, improving concentration, and increasing self-awareness. There are many different forms of meditation. Some of the more well-known types are comprised of the following:

5.2. Yoga and Tai Chi

Movement has been found to be an effective method for changing the mood and is the primary goal of the first portion of a yoga class. Yoga has been effective in the treatment of depression by increasing serotonin levels and decreasing monoamine oxidase levels. Low levels of GABA have been associated with anxiety and depression. Yoga increases GABA, resulting in improved mood and decreased anxiety.

The stress response in the body has been shown to cause a release of chemicals that affect the immune system and slow wound healing. The stress response has been linked to heart disease, cancer, and immune-mediated disease. The immune system is suppressed during depression, anxiety, and other negative emotional states, which in turn can increase the risk of illness. Chronic stress and negative emotional states commonly cause a host of other health issues. Yoga and tai chi have been of interest to researchers studying the effects of stress on the body. These mind-body interventions have been shown to benefit the body by lowering the activity of the stress response and by increasing relaxation response activity. This is accomplished by a number of physiological mechanisms.

5.3. Energy Healing

William Browne has done a wonderful job in describing stages of energy healing: "Energy healing takes a holistic view of the patient, considering the complex interplay of mind, body, and spirit. It uses energy as a tool or a medium of understanding and focuses on rebalancing the patient's energy and returning it to a state of balance." He describes that there are various healing modalities that utilize an energy system, such as acupuncture, reiki, homeopathy, and crystal therapy, to name a few. Each modality uses different techniques to influence the energy system. This can be done from anything to placing crystals on certain parts of the body to needle placement at acupuncture points. Despite the difference in technique, all energy healing modalities are working towards the same goal of balancing the energy system. Once the energy system is balanced, the effect should filter through to the patient's mind and body.

Understanding what Ψ means - spirit, mind, and energy - is foundational for understanding holistic healing and for reviews such as this one. The human being is not just a physical body, but a composite of energy, emotion, and mind. Being holistic healing deals with bringing balance to the energy system, which in turn will affect the mind and body associated with the energy system. Healers within many healing modalities have come to appreciate the importance of working with the energy body to affect change.

CHAPTER 6

Nutrition and Holistic Health

Once individuals start to become aware of their own health and the positive changes they can make, they often become interested in holistic medicine and how to maintain their well-being. This is commonly known as nutritional medicine, where health professionals and experts use diet and supplements to promote wellness. It is a way for individuals to take more responsibility for their own health and healing, and it is becoming more widely recognized and used in the field of healthcare. The new approach to healing involves learning how to prevent illness, how to stay healthy, and how to incorporate these practices into everyday life. By doing so, individuals can achieve optimal health and prevent chronic conditions from developing. The increasing prevalence of chronic diseases and degenerative conditions highlights the importance of taking proactive measures to improve health. Those who are serious about transforming their health and reducing healthcare costs may seek guidance from healthcare professionals who specialize in holistic medicine. From a professional standpoint, the goal is to help patients reduce symptoms and improve overall function. This approach is particularly appealing to individuals who are proactive and positive about their health. People in their late 30s to 60s who want to prevent disability and maintain an active lifestyle can benefit from holistic medicine.

6.1. Organic and Whole Foods

Gerson remedy sufferers may be familiar with the advice of consuming only organic meals. Dr. Gerson said that salt and chemicals used for extra processing of canned and frozen meals disable the body's natural healing mechanisms. He felt keenly that it is most beneficial to consume food that has been grown with vitamins and care, and was an avid and vocal fan of utilizing the therapeutic properties of fruits and vegetables that were grown organically.

People who are allergic to preservatives, chemicals, and food colorings are suggested to only eat organic meals. Consuming a lot of these chemicals can worsen the allergic response, as many produced foods contain adjunct agents that can act as potentiators for allergic reactions.

This can help lessen the chance of consuming toxins and components that can be hazardous to health while eating natural produce that is rich in nutrients. It has also been suggested that meals grown with artificial fertilizers and insecticides leach the soil of precious minerals. This has led to the fact that US fruit and greens of today comprise lesser nutrient content than it did 50 years ago.

6.2. Superfoods and Nutritional Supplements

Superfoods and nutritional supplements have made their way into health food stores, along with wild claims of curing and preventing illness. Although some of these claims are true, it is not the superfood itself that is the cause of healing, but the nutrition that the superfood provides. Let's face it, most of America is not consuming a diet that prevents many illnesses. This is evident with the growing obesity rates. Hence, the phrase 'prevention is the best medicine' rings true. What most people do not understand is that illness often is the result of deficiencies and imbalances in the body. The logical solution to this problem is through consumption of a balanced diet. Our diet should be the first thing we seek to change when our bodies are in a state of disease. While there are some fantastic superfoods and supplements that we can take to usher in healing, they are best serving their purpose as a compliment to a healthy diet.

6.3. Detoxification and Cleansing

A detoxification and cleansing program may consist of a special diet, herbs and supplements, hydrotherapy, exercise, breathing techniques, and/or sauna. Detoxification is also helpful for the treatment of chronic infections or immune diseases. Conditions like immune disease can be caused by a buildup of toxins, and a detoxification program can help the body in ridding these toxins.

Detoxification and cleansing are used to help remove toxins, which are substances that can be harmful to the body. Detoxification is a natural process that the body does to get rid of dangerous substances. The liver is known to be the key organ in the body's detoxification processes. Traditionally, detoxification means cleaning the blood. This is done by removing impurities from the blood in the liver, where toxins are processed for elimination. The body also eliminates toxins through the kidneys, intestines, lungs, lymph, and skin. But when these systems are compromised, impurities aren't properly filtered and the toxic load in the body increases.

CHAPTER 7

Integrating Alternative Therapies with Conventional Medicine

7.1. Collaborative Approach to Healing explains that concurrent treatment by conventional and alternative healthcare providers requires a high level of understanding between the patient and all the practitioners involved. The patient is essentially the one in the driver's seat and it is up to the patient to make decisions that will have a strong impact on the various treatments. Open communication between all the practitioners is essential. Holistic Healing offers an easy-to-understand Medical Decision Making Grid found in the next section which can be a useful tool for patients to coordinate their various treatments with less confusion.

Holistic Healing: A comprehensive guide to alternative therapies discusses how to work integratively with alternative and complementary therapies. It emphasizes that communication is essential between the conventional and alternative therapists so that there is proper understanding of the treatment and the potential side effects. The goal of this integrated treatment is to facilitate the self-healing process while maintaining support and symptomatic relief for the patient. It is recognized that no one system of medicine has all the tools to deal with every possible health issue. The different systems of medicine have their own unique strengths and weaknesses. An integrative approach applies the best possible tool to fix a specific health problem while minimizing any risk to the patient. This should result in a high therapeutic yield with a low incidence of adverse effects.

7.1. Collaborative Approach to Healing

The simple chart further illustrates how integrative medicine aims to combine teachings of modern and traditional medicine to what it deems as most effective relief. This notion provides a stark contrast to what is considered possible if compared to Western medicine and just traditional medicine. This aim to provide a patient with proactive and preventative treatment while providing capabilities for coping with current health issues is just not possible if using just traditional or modern medicinal techniques.

This definition gives the average person a solid understanding by stating what integrative medicine is, what it aims to achieve, and how it will go about achieving said aims. The use of the term "thoughtful combination" is an effective way to demonstrate that integrative medicine is not just hastily putting two types of medicine together but rather taking time to analyze and combine the best elements of both into a comprehensive healthcare plan.

Integrative medicine is a term still very much misunderstood, but the Hay article provides a comprehensive yet simplistic definition. "Integrative medicine is the thoughtful combination of complementary or alternative medicine with conventional biomedicine. It is an evolution in the practice of medicine that better addresses the healthcare needs of the 21st century. By combining numerous healing systems, integrative medicine offers a strategy that brings forth the best of each medicine, and each professional, to the patient."

By now, many patients and healthcare professionals alike would be dissuaded by the idea of integrating any "alternative" therapies with conventional medicine. However, discussing the combining of modern and traditional medicinal techniques is now an effective way to provide effective healthcare to all individuals.

7.2. Complementary Treatments

Complementary treatments may be used to help in the side effects of cancer or cancer treatment, to bring relief to the symptoms, and to improve the quality of life during cancer treatment and cancer survivorship. They say that helping the patient to heal, thrive, and survive may also be considered as cancer treatments. An example of treatment that is aimed at cancer survival is the use of antioxidants to neutralize the free radicals that are harmful to healthy cells. It is also important to discuss your symptoms and the side effects of your conventional cancer treatments with your physicians before choosing and pursuing a complementary treatment. This is an effort to obtain effective conventional and best cancer treatments. This also allows your doctor to make sure that a given CAM approach or cancer treatment will not compromise cancer care or cancer treatment.

7.3. Managing Side Effects

Taste alterations – Eat cold foods such as sandwiches or fruit salads. Avoid sweet-tasting foods if treatment has caused a sweet taste in the mouth. Try tart foods if you have a metallic taste in your mouth. Use plastic utensils if food now tastes metallic.

Fatigue – Increase fluid for adequate hydration. Small, frequent meals may help to maintain energy levels. Light exercise may help to increase energy.

Constipation – Increase fluid intake. Drink warm liquids in the morning. Eat high-fiber cereal and include fresh or dried fruit or beans and lentils in at least two meals per day.

Diarrhea – Increase fluid intake to 8-10 glasses of caffeine-free liquid per day. Eat high pectin foods such as peaches, apples, oranges, and grapefruit. Decrease insoluble fiber intake from whole grain products and vegetables.

Nausea/vomiting – Take foods and drinks at room temperature. Avoid sweet, fried, and fatty foods. Ginger may help to relieve nausea.

In order to manage the side effects of conventional treatments, it is important to consume the right nutrition. A wide range of side effects could be lessened through effective and safe supplement or dietary modification. Listed below are common side effects of conventional treatments and recommended nutrition guidelines.

CHAPTER 8

Holistic Healing for Specific Conditions

Naturopathy is also an effective system for pain management. Consider if the pain is worse in some weather conditions, at different times of day, or if it is associated with other symptoms and factors. This information gives clues to the root causes of the pain and factors affecting it. For example, pain and stiffness that is worse in cold and damp weather is typically a result of cold and dampness lodging in the body. Or pain that comes and goes in a fixed location, and is quite severe, can be caused by bi syndrome and is due to a wind condition in the channels.

Pain is also best addressed in a holistic manner using a combination of therapies, including acupuncture, herbal medicine, and diet and lifestyle changes. Regardless of the duration and type of pain, we believe that pain is the result of the body not being in balance, and it's our job to diagnose the imbalance and correct it. This may involve looking much further than the painful site, and we will often treat conditions seemingly unrelated to the pain in order to restore overall balance. An example might be a sharp pain in the ribcage as a result of liver qi stagnation or a person with painful arthritic knees exhibiting signs of kidney yang deficiency.

Pain alone is the most common reason for consulting a complementary and alternative medicine practitioner – and it's one condition that science has shown can be helped by the use of acupuncture. Acupuncture is the chosen method for pain management for many difficult to diagnose and hard to manage conditions, and for those seeking drug-free alternatives.

8.1. Pain Management

Let's illustrate here the difference between holistic, homeostatic pain management and a conventional approach. The conventional medical approach to the reduction of pain is to isolate the symptom and treat it with analgesics or a series of prescribed exercises without seeking to understand the cause of pain. The holistic approach recognises that pain is a symptom of an imbalance in the body and seeks to address the underlying cause through a variety of methods and thereby restore harmony to the individual. This is essentially a form of homeostasis as pain is an indication that the body is in an unbalanced state. Pain is very subjective and often difficult to measure, and if it becomes chronic it can have a very detrimental effect on an individual's quality of life. The ability to effectively manage and reduce pain through holistic therapy can prevent the need for surgical procedures and a lifetime of prescription drugs. By recognising the holistic approach to pain management, perhaps there is potential for a considerable saving on healthcare costs.

8.2. Stress and Anxiety

Cognitive Behavior Therapy is also a very effective treatment for stress and anxiety. This form of therapy helps persons to understand and change the behavior and thoughts that cause the feelings of anxiety. Unfortunately for many, the key to relaxation is in the form of a sedative medication. This is not a healthy or viable long-term solution, but in the short term, it can be very beneficial for some at breaking a cycle of chronic anxiety. More healthy and reliable long-term chemical relief has been found with an amino acid called Gaba. Gaba works as a mild tranquilizer and is the primary inhibitory neurotransmitter in the brain. Studies have shown that low levels of Gaba are linked to high levels of anxiety and that raising Gaba levels can effectively reduce anxiety. Gaba levels can be increased by prescription medication or by using natural methods such as meditation and an intake of more magnesium.

People with chronic stress and anxiety often have a very hard time trying to relax. There are many steps and methods for relaxation, and with persistence and creativity, the majority of persons can find a method that works for them. Some try stretching. Others try a hobby, like gardening. There are those that simply put their feet up and watch their favorite TV show. Often times a vacation or a change of occupation is necessary. It is very important to identify the activities and situations that increase stress and either avoid them or figure out a way to deal with them in a manner that is healthier.

Stress and anxiety affect everyone, and modern society has become an unlikely breeding ground for this noxious pair. The brisk pace, constant demands, the dehumanization of education and workplace, even the ever-pressuring threat of potential terrorist attacks - all play a part. Persons suffering from stress and anxiety may feel edgy and tired, be easily frustrated, forgetful, unable to concentrate, and as previously mentioned may have an increased heart and breathing rate. Fortunately for these persons and unfortunately for the rest of us, stress and anxiety are highly treatable conditions. The same lifestyle that spawns stress and anxiety often times supplies the cure; it is a simple thing called relaxation.

8.3. Insomnia and Sleep Disorders

Many sleep-promoting herbs work by increasing the levels of specific neurotransmitters that are involved in initiating and maintaining sleep. Other herbs work by reducing anxiety, which can be a root cause of insomnia but which often goes undetected as a cause for sleeplessness. Herbal treatments are gently effective and it is usually quite safe to experiment with them. If you are already taking medications, you should consult your doctor before embarking on a course of herbal remedies to make sure that there are no adverse interactions.

For thousands of years, across continents and cultures, people have trusted in traditional herbal remedies to address a wide variety of health problems. Sleep disorders are no exception. Many cultures have a long history of using herbs to treat disturbed sleep patterns, dreams, and nightmares. It only stands to reason that, in an era of increasing drug resistance and awareness of the potential side effects of synthetic medications, interest in herbal treatment of sleep problems is on the rise.

8.4. Digestive Issues

A research paper investigates the application of holistic healing techniques to the specific symptom of epigastric pain in people with a wide range of functional gastrointestinal disorders. The paper recommends a comprehensive assessment of dietary intake for patients with epigastric pain, keeping a food diary, and doing an elimination diet. This aims to identify if there are any specific foods that are triggering symptoms. The paper states that food allergy and intolerance are common causes of epigastric pain and functional bowel problems, and that a trial of a low allergen or specific carbohydrate diet may often help. Herbal medicine and acupuncture also have a fairly strong evidence base in the management of functional gastrointestinal disorders.

Functional dyspepsia is thought to be a disturbance in the way the stomach and intestines digest food. However, it is still unclear about the exact pathophysiology of this disease and risk factors such as diet, genetics, stress, and medication may all play a part. Abnormalities in gastrointestinal motility, visceral hypersensitivity, altered gut immunity, and the presence of Helicobacter Pylori in the stomach have also been implicated.

Dyspepsia is a functional disease that affects about 20% of Americans and can be defined by a number of signs and symptoms in the upper gastrointestinal tract. The broad term of dyspepsia incorporates a huge variety of symptoms including bloating, burping, nausea, anorexia, and a sense of fullness after eating. People with dyspepsia often feel that they have a constant sore stomach and can be in a lot of pain. This pain can vary in severity and be experienced by the patient as burning, gnawing, aching or sharp. The symptoms can develop and get worse, limiting the amount of daily functioning someone can perform.

8.5. Immune System Support

In general, it is best to have an idea of the sort of outcome you desire before starting. (This works for most things in life!) For boosting the immune system, the ideal is to prevent the onset of illness altogether. However, if you are someone who always succumbs to illness or you suffer from a chronic condition, prevention of illness may not seem like a realistic outcome. In this case, it would be beneficial to focus more on managing the illness and working to reduce the severity and longevity of symptoms. At worst, you may aim to prevent a worsening of your condition. All of these types of goals are realistic and are tailored at the individual level. It is beneficial to have thought of a specific goal, as this can keep you on track and provide motivation. With a clear goal, success can be highly motivating and improving your health can become a self-perpetuating process.

CHAPTER 9

Finding the Right Practitioner

Once you have chosen a practitioner, whether it is a medical doctor or a complementary and alternative medicine practitioner, it is important that you feel comfortable with him or her. A practitioner/client relationship is a partnership, and it is essential that both parties feel at ease. Always trust your instincts; if something doesn't feel quite right, keep looking.

Word of mouth is often the best way to find a good practitioner, so ask people you know if they can recommend someone. If you have been prescribed a treatment from a book or a website, try contacting the authors to see whether they can recommend a practitioner in your area. Some professional organizations may be able to provide a list of practitioners who meet their specific criteria. This information can often be obtained by sending a self-addressed, stamped envelope to the organization.

There are a number of ways to find the right practitioner. When looking for a new practitioner, most people want to know about the practitioner's training and experience. Learning whether or not the practitioner has treated conditions similar to yours and how successful he or she was in treating them can be very helpful. Also, be sure to know whether the practitioner is willing to work alongside your allopathic (conventional) physician. He or she may be the best practitioner in the world, but if he or she does not communicate with your doctor, there could be problems.

9.1. Researching Credentials and Experience

When we talk about alternative therapies, knowledge and experience consistently come out as important factors. It is important for us to know where the healer or practitioner gets their knowledge and experience. What method or therapy do they offer? The knowledge of some knowledge about the therapy is important so the healer can explain the process and the result of the therapy to you. It is also important for us to know the success rate of the therapy that they offer. We also want to know if the healer has experience with the same case as ours and what the result of the therapy that they do. This information will give us more confidence and trust in the healer. If the healer is still active in improving their knowledge and skills, it means that we can expect a good result from their therapy.

Researching a practitioner's credentials and experience is important. The feeling of a spiritual healer should also be comfortable, and we should build good communication with him. Many holistic and alternative medical treatments are offered by people who aren't licensed medical practitioners. Among conventional medical doctors as well, a board-certified specialist has more expertise in a given field than a generalist. A practitioner's experience with a medical condition is important, although years of experience may not be as significant as how recently the practitioner has dealt with the condition and how often. A good question to ask any practitioner is how effective they feel they have been with that condition.

9.2. Seeking Recommendations and Referrals

Referrals can be quite a safe way of finding a good practitioner, although bear in mind that what helped one person with their specific condition may not necessarily help another. Often, word of mouth is the best way of finding out about a particular practitioner's success rate in treating a specific condition. You may have a colleague at work who had hypnotherapy to stop smoking and found it highly successful. This would be a good opportunity to find out more about the hypnotherapist. A good family doctor should also know something about the success rate of various treatments that their patients have undertaken and may be able to suggest a suitable therapy and/or practitioner.

When seeking referrals or recommendations for an alternative therapy practitioner, there can be important things to consider. Did the person giving the referral have a similar health problem to yours? If so, did the practitioner have a good success rate in treating that condition? If your friend had a great result from a practitioner for a non-specific condition such as stress, it might not be so relevant to your condition of migraines. Gather as much information as possible about the treatment the practitioner gave and how the person giving the referral felt about the practitioner's manner and effectiveness.

9.3. Trusting Your Instincts

Sometimes you may consider ending the therapy if the therapy process is not meeting your needs. An instinct that the therapy is not as effective as it should be is a good reason to look into other forms of therapy or to talk to the practitioner about altering the current one. This type of decision should be made after carefully thought out consideration and weighing the pros and cons. Be sure to discuss this with the practitioner to get his or her opinion on the matter. Remember that your instincts are a powerful tool and it is important to trust them. Any doubts about the practitioner, therapy, or concerns about your wellbeing should be discussed with the practitioner. Open communication, trusting your instincts, and careful consideration will ensure that you make the right decision concerning your holistic therapy.

During the therapy process, ask yourself if the practitioner is dependable and reliable. Does the person promptly return phone calls or address any concerns you may have? If the person missed an appointment, did they provide an adequate explanation? These are signs of the practitioner's professionalism and competence. If you feel uncomfortable with the person's dependability, it may be time to discuss your concerns with the practitioner or to consider ending the therapy.

Your instincts can reveal a lot about the practitioner and the therapy. They will help you to make the final decision about the practitioner, whether it is to continue with the therapy, or when to stop. When you first meet the practitioner, take notice of your first impressions. Do you feel comfortable talking with him or her? Is the practitioner a good listener? Does he or she seem genuinely concerned about your well-being? Does the person seem trustworthy? What is your gut feeling about this person? First impressions are very telling, so take heed to what your instincts are telling you.

CHAPTER 10

Incorporating Holistic Healing into Your Lifestyle

With much effort and determination, a wellness routine can be a life-changing experience that will set the path to a happy and healthy life. Step-by-step instructions for creating a wellness routine and examples of what a routine looks like can be found on the National Wellness Institute website.

The last step is to make a commitment to yourself to follow through with your routine and achieve your goals. Writing a self-contract is an effective way to make this commitment, and posting your goals in a place where you will see them every day serves as a constant reminder of what you are trying to achieve.

Once you have set clear goals for your routine, it is important to explore and learn about the various ways holistic healing practices can help you achieve these goals. The next step is to create a schedule for implementing these practices into your life and sticking to it. Often times, it helps to work with a holistic practitioner to guide you in the right direction and visit periodically to monitor your progress.

Creating a Wellness Routine A wellness routine is a coordinated effort to achieve a desired state of mind and body by focusing on prevention and self-education. The first step in creating a wellness routine is to make a list of health goals that you would like to achieve. These goals will be the focus of your routine and can be related to preventing illness or improving overall well-being.

Now that you have learned about the various alternative therapies and how they can benefit your mind, body, and spirit, you are probably wondering how you can incorporate these therapies into your day-to-day life. Creating a daily and weekly routine that focuses on preventing illness and improving overall well-being is one of the easiest and most effective ways to make holistic healing practices a part of your lifestyle.

10.1. Creating a Wellness Routine

A wellness routine is a series of activities or steps that you take part in regularly to increase your level of health and wellbeing. The objective of a wellness routine is to increase one's level of health in all areas of life - mental, physical, emotional, etc. - by using preventative measures, being educated about one's health, and making healthy choices. At first, changing your lifestyle to include a wellness routine can be difficult, but by keeping your goals in mind and planning for small steps to reach them, you can make this change more manageable and successful. Your wellness routine is to be designed by and for you. It should be something unique to your needs and goals. Keep in mind that improving your health is a marathon, not a sprint, so be kind to yourself and patient in implementing your routine.

10.2. Self-Care Practices

The practice of good sleep hygiene: In these modern times, disturbed sleep patterns and insomnia are becoming more and more common. It is now recognized that long-term sleep deprivation can lead to many chronic health conditions. Getting good sleep can be a complex issue, but practicing good sleep hygiene is the first step to overcoming sleep problems. Measures can include reducing caffeine intake, going to bed earlier, establishing a pre-sleep routine, and ensuring the sleep environment is dark and free from noise and interruptions.

Spiritual connection: Regardless of religious affiliation, spiritual connection can provide a greater sense of purpose and meaning in life. This can contribute to a sense of hope and optimism. Spiritual connection can be achieved through religious practices, meditation, quiet reflection time, nature walks, and finding a connection with others.

Exercise: Regular physical activity has several proven benefits for overall health and treating chronic illness. Physical activity can help to maintain a healthy weight and reduce blood pressure - two key factors in preventing disease process. Regular physical activity can also help improve mood and feelings of well-being. Exercise is a well-known therapy for depression and anxiety. Holistic forms of exercise such as yoga and tai chi can also promote a sense of relaxation and reduce stress.

The most fundamental form of self-care always begins with being attentive to one's own healthcare. This means believing in and acknowledging the significance that diet, exercise, adequate water intake, sunlight, fresh air, rest, healthy relationships, and regular medical check-ups play in promoting healthy living. But it also extends to other self-care practices that involve more conscious, self-initiated activities.

10.3. Maintaining Balance and Harmony

Many people lead such unbalanced, off-kilter lives that they barely recognize what it's like to live in a state of equilibrium. Inner balance is a concept that is deep and wide and encompasses a multitude of ideas. However, basically it is the ability to remain present to your experience, whatever it is. It is also keeping a sense of steadiness and harmony in the midst of life's daily experiences. But being balanced does not mean being rigid and unchanging. You are able to be flexible and move with your life's experiences without being knocked over by them. It is not a trait that is easily obtained in today's society with its ever-changing and fast pace. Because balance is an inner state, it must be first cultivated and then nurtured. The desire to attain and maintain a balanced state of being must be strong enough to effect a change in your current way of living. You must experience the state of balance in order to know its value, and to do this, you will need some specific tools and activities to help you create balance in your life. Remember that a tool is only as good as the person who is using it, and to effectively use these tools to create balance in your life, you must have the motivation to be balanced and the willingness to self-reflect.

CHAPTER 11

Conclusion

The main purpose of this essay has been to issue a wake-up call in the hearts of all those who read it. In the final analysis, there is only one healer. That healer is within. The word healer comes from the Old English word "haelen" meaning "to make whole". Healers are those that help others to heal themselves. What greater gift and what greater service can there be? An understanding of the steps of the healing process may well be an essential part of the knowledge which all holistic therapists will need in the challenging years that lie ahead for the medicine of the whole person.

Throughout this essay, we have been describing a healing process which occurs over time and often in phases. If you have persisted in reading this far, it is possible that you have recognized, maybe for the first time, that one or other of your own illnesses is, in fact, a catalyst for change. Making contact with the real you, who is whole, spiritual, complete, and perfect, can involve even the greatest journey of a lifetime. This essay suggests that just maybe, one gleaming aspect of the real you is the healer. Should you be able to grasp the verity of this, then simply by being a more whole and healed individual, you will have helped many others. And often in ways...

9 798330 608300